Cooking with Wilson

Quick Kid-Friendly Recipes

Amanda Farwick

To Wilson, our sous chef extraordinaire.
The one who inspires us in all that we do
and brings great joy to everyone he meets.
May you always be an inspiration to others.

ISBN: 979-8998543203

Photography by Steve Farwick
Produced by Publish Pros | publishpros.com

Our son, Wilson, was born with Down syndrome and had early intervention, speech, physical, and occupational therapies from a young age. His therapists would tell us to have him pretend to stir, or grab objects with tongs, or to work with him to stand on and step up and down from a stool. Being someone who loves to cook, I thought, "Why not just have him actually help me stir, or serve food with tongs, while practicing getting up and down and standing on a stool?"

Our top priority for Wilson has always been for him to be as independent as possible. So, from the time he was about two years old he has been cooking with me. People are often amazed that we started cooking with a child with developmental delays at such a young age. Why not? When you think about it, cooking engages so many different skills—fine and gross motor skills are used for scooping, pouring, lifting and sorting bowls or ingredients, serving items with tongs, standing at the counter, cutting, opening packets, and measuring, just to name a few. Cooking together also provides the opportunity for math and speech development through sorting, counting, identifying objects and colors, following simple and multi-step directions, reading ingredients, and so much more.

I am not a therapist or a chef. I am just a mama who loves to cook and wants to help her son gain as much independence and learn as many life skills as possible. In this cookbook, I share with you some of the recipes Wilson most enjoys helping me with. I encourage you to start cooking with your children and discover what they enjoy making.

It's time to get messy, be creative, and have fun learning together in the kitchen!

Amanda Farwick

Baked Apples

Ingredients

- 4 large apples
- 2 tablespoons salted butter, softened
- ¼ cup brown sugar
- ¼ cup quick cook oats
- ½ teaspoon ground cinnamon
- ¼ teaspoon ground nutmeg
- 1 teaspoon vanilla extract
- ½ cup water

Directions

1. Wash and remove core from apples.

2. Fill an 8-inch x 8-inch ungreased baking dish with ½ cup water and stand apples up in dish.

3. Use a fork to mix together the remaining ingredients in a separate bowl.

4. Fill apples with oatmeal mixture.

5. Bake at 350° for 30-45 minutes or until apples are soft.

Servings: 4

BUTTER

NET WT. 13.4 g

Mini Banana Pudding

Ingredients

- 5 ounces instant vanilla pudding
- 2 cups whole milk
- 14 ounces sweetened condensed milk
- 1 tablespoon vanilla extract
- 16 ounces thawed whipped cream
- ½ box vanilla wafers
- 3 bananas, sliced
- 4 mini trifle cups or 10-ounce serving cups of your choice

Directions

1. Mix together pudding and whole milk.

2. Stir in sweetened condensed milk and vanilla extract.

3. Gently stir in half of the whipped cream.

4. Add one layer of vanilla wafers, banana slices, and pudding mixture to each serving dish.

5. Repeat layers until dishes are full.

6. Top with remaining whipped cream and crushed wafers.

Servings: 4

BBQ Chicken Flatbread

Ingredients

- 1 naan flatbread, approximately 9 inches x 7 inches
- 1 cup rotisserie chicken
- ¼ cup thinly sliced red onion
- ¼ cup banana pepper rings
- 1 tablespoon olive oil
- 1 teaspoon garlic powder
- 1 cup shredded mozzarella or pepper jack cheese
- 2 tablespoons bbq sauce

Directions

1. Dice chicken into small pieces.
2. Brush olive oil on flatbread and sprinkle with garlic powder.
3. Top flatbread with cheese, shredded chicken, red onion, and banana peppers.
4. Bake according to flatbread directions.
5. Drizzle with bbq sauce after baking.

Servings: 2

Charcuterie Cups

Ingredients (per cup)

- ¼ cup any type of nuts
- 1 ounce mozzarella cheese stick
- 1 cheese wedge, about 0.5 ounces
- 1 ounce beef stick broken in half
- 2 cherry tomatoes
- 1 mini pickle
- 1 peeled mandarin orange
- 1 mini bell pepper
- 1 breadstick
- Individual 12 ounce serving cup of your choice

Directions

1. Fill bottom of cup with nuts.
2. Place breadstick, cheese stick and beef stick in back of cup.
3. Fill in with smaller items along front and sides until cup is full.
4. Get creative with your ingredients and placement.

Yield: 1 cup

Corn Dog Bites

Ingredients

- 1 8.5 ounce box corn muffin mix (plus ingredients listed on package)
- 4 hot dogs, uncooked
- Cooking spray

Directions

1. Make corn muffin mixture according to package directions.
2. Cut each hot dog into 6 equal pieces.
3. Spray mini muffin pan with cooking spray.
4. Add batter to each mini muffin cup until about three-fourths full.
5. Press one piece of hot dog into each cup.
6. Bake at 400° for 8-12 minutes or until golden brown.

Yield: 24 bites

Frozen Fruit & Yogurt Pops

Ingredients

Strawberry Pops

- 2 cups frozen strawberries
- ¼ cup lime juice
- ¼ cup honey
- ¼ cup water

Blueberry Yogurt Pops

- 1 cup vanilla Greek yogurt
- 1 ½ cups frozen blueberries
- 2 tablespoons honey
- ¼ cup milk

Yield: 6 of each flavor

Directions

1. Blend ingredients for each type of pop separately in food processor until well combined.

2. Pour into 7.5 inch popsicle sleeves.

3. Freeze for at least 1 hour.

Simple Hummus

Ingredients

- 15 ounces canned chickpeas (drain and save liquid)
- 1 tablespoon olive oil
- 1 tablespoon lemon juice
- ½ teaspoon ground cumin
- ½ teaspoon minced garlic
- ¼ teaspoon salt

Directions

1. Blend all ingredients in food processor until well combined.
2. Add chickpea liquid to desired consistency.
3. Chill in refrigerator for at least 2 hours before serving.

Servings: 4

Loaded Pretzels

Ingredients

- 12 ounce bag pretzel rods
- 8 ounce bag caramel bits
- 1 cup toffee bits (not chocolate covered)
- ½ cup salted pecan pieces
- 1 cup peanut butter chips
- 1 cup mini chocolate chips

Directions

1. Break pretzel rods in half.
2. Mix toffee bits, pecans, peanut butter, and chocolate chips and spread on a plate.
3. Melt caramel according to package directions.
4. Dip broken ends of pretzel rods about one third of the way into melted caramel, then roll in toppings, pressing gently until they stick.
5. Cool on waxed paper.

Yield: Approximately 36

Mac & Cheese Cups

Ingredients

- ½ box of elbow noodles, cooked and drained
- 3 cups shredded cheddar cheese
- 1 cup milk
- 2 tablespoons melted butter
- 1 beaten egg
- ½ teaspoon black pepper
- Cooking spray

Directions

1. Mix all ingredients except cooking spray together, saving about 1 cup of cheese for topping.

2. Spray a regular sized muffin pan with cooking spray.

3. Scoop ingredients into muffin pan, filling each one.

4. Sprinkle remaining cheese on top of each cup.

5. Bake at 350° for 25 minutes.

Yield: 12 cups

Meatball Pockets

Ingredients

- 8 canned biscuits, regular size
- 16 cooked meatballs
- 4 mozzarella cheese sticks cut into 4 pieces each
- 2 tablespoons olive oil
- 1 teaspoon garlic powder
- 1 teaspoon Italian seasoning
- 1 tablespoon grated parmesan cheese
- Cooking spray

Directions

1. Coat 9-inch round pan with cooking spray.
2. Break biscuits in half, making two circles.
3. Place a piece of cheese and a meatball in the middle of each biscuit.
4. Pinch to seal each biscuit.
5. Place biscuits in pan, sealed side down, until pan is full.
6. Brush tops of biscuits with olive oil and sprinkle with parmesan cheese, garlic powder, and Italian seasoning.
7. Bake at 350° for about 15 minutes or until brown.

Yield: 16 pockets

Oatmeal Bake

Ingredients

- 2 cups quick cook oats
- 2 tablespoons maple syrup or honey
- 1 ½ cups milk
- 1 cup chopped apples or ½ cup raisins
- 1 egg
- 1 teaspoon vanilla extract
- 1 tablespoon olive oil
- 2 teaspoons pumpkin pie spice
- ¼ cup chopped pecans or walnuts
- Cooking spray

Directions

1. Coat 8 x 8 inch pan with cooking spray.
2. Stir all ingredients together.
3. Pour into prepared pan.
4. Bake at 350° for 45 minutes.
5. Cut into squares and serve with extra honey or syrup drizzled on top. It is even great to reheat the next day.

Servings: 4

Party Popcorn

Ingredients

- 2 bags microwave popcorn, popped
- 12 ounce bag candy melts in your favorite color
- 2 tablespoons sprinkles

Directions

1. Remove any unpopped kernels of popcorn.
2. Spread popcorn in a layer on wax paper.
3. Melt candy melts per package directions and drizzle over popcorn.
4. Gently stir until popcorn is coated with melted candy.
5. Top with your favorite sprinkles.

Servings: 6

Peanut Butter Cookies

Ingredients

- 1 cup granulated sugar
- 1 cup brown sugar
- 1 cup peanut butter
- 1 cup salted butter, softened
- 2 eggs
- 1 teaspoon vanilla extract
- 1 teaspoon baking soda
- 1 teaspoon baking powder
- 3 cups all-purpose flour
- Cooking spray or parchment paper

Directions

1. Mix butter and sugars until well combined.

2. Add peanut butter, eggs, and vanilla extract.

3. Mix together dry ingredients in separate bowl.

4. Add dry ingredients to liquid ingredients and mix well.

5. Line cookie sheet with parchment paper or coat with cooking spray.

6. Scoop 12 cookies onto prepared cookie sheet using a 2-tablespoon cookie scoop.

7. Dip fork in water and press into each cookie twice to create a crosshatch pattern.

8. Bake at 350° for 10-12 minutes.

Yield: 3 dozen (ish)

FLOUR
100% ORGANIC
BROWN SUGAR

Spray your measuring cup with cooking spray before measuring peanut butter and it won't stick.

Wilson ♡

Pimento Cheese

Ingredients

- 4 ounce block extra-sharp cheddar cheese
- 4 ounce block mild cheddar cheese
- 4 ounce jar diced pimento peppers, undrained
- 1 cup mayonnaise
- Black pepper and cayenne pepper (optional)

Directions

1. Grate cheeses.
2. Stir pimentos with juice into cheeses.
3. Stir in mayonnaise.
4. Add a dash of pepper and/or cayenne to your taste.
5. Chill for at least 1 hour.

Servings: 4

TIP: You can use pre-shredded cheese, but freshly grated yields the best results.

Pizza Pinwheels

Ingredients

- 12 ounce pizza dough
- 1 cup pizza sauce
- 2 ½ cups shredded mozzarella cheese
- 30 slices pepperoni

Directions

1. Roll out pizza dough into a rectangle approximately 13 inches by 9 inches.

2. Top dough with sauce, cheese, and pepperoni.

3. Starting with the long side, roll the topped dough into a log and cut into twelve 1-inch pieces.

4. Stand each piece up in a regular sized greased muffin pan.

5. Bake at 350° for 10-12 minutes or until brown.

6. Serve with leftover pizza sauce for dipping.

Yield: 12 pinwheels

Sandwich Skewers

Ingredients

- 8 sandwich bread slices
- 4 cheese slices
- 4 ham or turkey slices
- 16 cherry tomatoes
- 8 small or 4 large wooden skewers

Directions

1. Use your favorite cookie cutter to cut bread, cheese, and meat into shapes.

2. Build sandwiches with bread, meat, and cheese shapes.

3. Thread mini sandwiches onto skewers with a tomato between each sandwich.

Servings: 4

Don't like tomatoes? A pickle, olive, or piece of your favorite fruit works just as well.

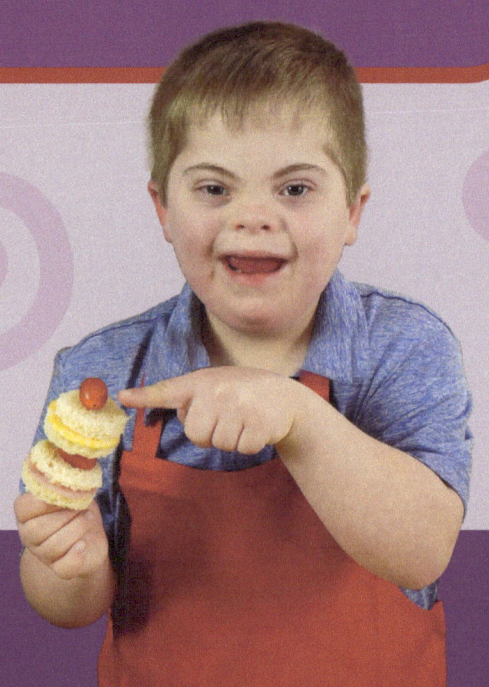

Seasoned Pretzels

Ingredients

- 1 pound pretzel twists or sticks
- ½ cup vegetable oil
- 1 packet dry ranch dressing mix
- 1 teaspoon garlic powder
- 1 teaspoon onion powder
- 1 teaspoon dried dill

Directions

1. Whisk seasonings into oil.
2. Pour seasoned oil into gallon bag with pretzels, shake to evenly coat.
3. Spread in single layer on ungreased baking sheet.
4. Bake at 350° for 10-12 minutes.

Yield: 16 ounces

Tin Foil Dinner

Ingredients

- 4 frozen meatballs
- ½ cup mixed frozen vegetables
- ¼ cup shredded cheddar cheese
- 6 frozen tater tots
- 14 inch aluminum foil square
- Cooking spray
- Your favorite seasonings, such as salt, pepper, garlic powder, Worcestershire sauce, or ketchup

Directions

1. Coat one side of foil with cooking spray.
2. Place meatballs, tater tots, and vegetables onto foil.
3. Top with cheese and your favorite seasonings.
4. Bring the longer two sides of foil together and fold down a few times to seal.
5. Fold each short end a few times toward the middle of the packet to seal.
6. Cook at 400° on grill or in oven for 30 minutes.
7. Open carefully to allow steam to release.

Servings: 1

Ultimate Cookies & Milk

Ingredients

- 1 13-ounce package chocolate chip cookies
- 2 cups whole milk
- 8 ounces thawed whipped cream

Directions

1. Quickly dunk one whole cookie in milk and place in 8-inch x 8-inch ungreased baking dish.

2. Repeat until bottom of dish is covered in cookies.

3. Top cookies with half of whipped cream.

4. Repeat steps.

5. Top second layer of whipped cream with leftover crushed cookies.

6. Allow to chill in refrigerator about 6 hours before eating.

Servings: 4

This is the first recipe I remember learning to make by myself when I was a kid.

Amanda

Wilson's Famous

Chocolate Chip Cookies

Ingredients

- ½ cup brown sugar
- ¼ cup granulated sugar
- ½ cup salted butter, softened
- 1 egg, room temperature
- 1 teaspoon vanilla extract
- 1 ½ cups all-purpose flour
- 1 teaspoon baking soda
- ¼ teaspoon salt
- 1 ⅓ cups chocolate chips, any kind or combination
- Cooking spray or parchment paper

Yield: 2 dozen (ish)

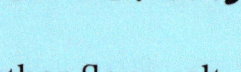

Directions

1. Stir together flour, salt, and baking soda and set aside.

2. Beat butter and sugars with mixer until well combined.

3. Add egg and vanilla to butter mixture and mix until blended.

4. Add flour mixture to butter mixture and mix until it forms a dough.

5. Add chocolate chips and mix into the dough.

6. Line cookie sheet with parchment paper or coat with cooking spray.

7. Scoop 12 cookies onto prepared cookie sheet using 2-tablespoon cookie scoop.

8. Chill scooped cookies in refrigerator 15 minutes before baking.

9. Bake at 350° for 10-12 minutes or until edges and tops start to brown.

Wilson prefers a mix of equal parts dark chocolate chunks, mini semi-sweet chips, and milk chocolate chips. Use whatever combination you like best!

Meet the Farwick Family

We are Steve, Amanda, and Wilson Farwick from Lexington, South Carolina.

Originally from Ohio, Steve loves to watch just about any type of sports, especially those that involve his Ohio State Buckeyes.

Amanda, a South Carolina native, is a quintessential southern girl when it comes to cooking and is our planner in chief.

Wilson is happiest when he is entertaining or helping with something. He takes pride in having a job to do.

When we aren't in the kitchen together, you will often find us spreading a positive message of inclusion as we work to educate others about those with differing abilities.

Our work together includes projects such as this cookbook, with special credit given to Wilson Farwick, our sous-chef and chief inspiration officer, and Steve Farwick, or "Daddy Steve" as Wilson calls him, our photographer.

Follow the Farwicks on Tik Tok (@FarwickFamily), Facebook (@FarwickFamily) Instagram (@TheFarwickFamily).